Teaching Social Behavior To Young Children

William C. Sheppard, Ph.D.
Department of Psychology
University of Oregon and
Educational Environments, Inc.

Steven B. Shank
Educational Environments, Inc.

Darla Wilson
Educational Environments, Inc.

Research Press
2612 North Mattis Avenue
Champaign, Illinois 61820

Teaching Social Behavior to Young Children
Copyright © 1973 by William C. Sheppard

Formerly *How to Be a Good Teacher:*
Training Social Behavior in Young Children
Copyright © 1972 by William C. Sheppard

ISBN 0-87822-110-7

Partial financial support for this project was provided by the Office of Child Development (O.C.D.) and the Office of Economic Opportunity (O.E.O.), Grant No. H9807, through Research for Better Schools, Ronald K. Parker, principal investigator. The opinions expressed in this publication do not necessarily reflect the position or policy of O.C.D. or O.E.O. and no official endorsement by these agencies should be inferred.

Contents

This manual is primarily intended
for teachers of young children,
although anyone involved
in the teaching-learning process
will find it useful.

Introduction

Opening the playroom door, Mrs. Canessa smiled at the sounds of children at play. She heard laughter, imitations of cars, trains, and animals, sounds of toys being pushed, pulled, and ridden on, and, what she was waiting for, "There's my mommy!" from her five-year-old Lita. Lita was a student in a successful preschool program. As usual, she had gone to school eagerly that morning, and her mother had promised to visit her later in the day.

Mrs. Canessa arrived during the free play period, a few minutes before the children would be served juice and cookies. Mary, the teacher, welcomed Mrs. Canessa and showed her where to sit in order to see all the children best. Mrs. Canessa knew that the children liked Mary, and that other teachers respected Mary's ability to handle children. Even though this was only the second week in Mary's class, the children already seemed more cooperative and more skillful in getting along with each other than ever before. Mrs. Canessa wanted to watch Mary—maybe she could learn some better ways to manage her own family.

Little Eric was sitting near a group of children, playing quietly with a puzzle, when Mary left Mrs. Canessa and walked over to him. She knelt beside him for a few moments, apparently discussing the funny animals in the puzzle. Mrs. Canessa heard her say, "You're playing very nicely, Eric," when a loud shriek jerked their attention to a sobbing child.

Brady had just hit another boy and had taken away his colored ball, which he was bouncing against the floor while the boy looked on tearfully. Mary quickly took the ball away from Brady, and took him to a chair near the wall on the far side of the room, saying, "Brady, we do not hit here. If you hit, you can't play with the other children. Sit here until I say you can get up." Mrs. Canessa noted that Mary did not seem particularly upset with Brady or raise her voice at him, but talked to him in a firm, calm, matter-of-fact tone.

1

Brady's distressed victim got his ball back and went off bouncing it past four-year-old Robert, who was studiously building a tower of blocks. Mrs. Canessa watched him add block upon block until the tower teetered precariously. Suddenly the blocks clattered to the floor, and Robert whined unhappily. Mrs. Canessa saw Mary glance at Robert, then turn back to the other children. Presently, Robert began gathering up his blocks again.

Mrs. Canessa heard Mary speaking and looked over. Janet had just let Terry look through the plastic magnifying glass she had been playing with, and they had decided to take turns with it. Mary was saying, "Janet, it's very kind of you to share the magnifying glass with Terry. Here are some leaves—it may be fun to look closely at their veins through the glass."

Clatter! Robert's blocks had fallen over again. But this time, Mrs. Canessa noticed, he did not whine, but began right away to pick them up and rebuild his tower. Mary quickly walked over, touched Robert on the shoulder and said, "I like the way you are working, Robert."

"Mommy! Look! This is fun!" Lita and Johnny were spinning a musical top that swirled in a bright flash of color and played, "Mary Had a Little Lamb." Mary laughed with them at the pretty toy. She bent down to Johnny.

"Are you and Lita sharing the top?"

"Yes! We're making it go fast!"

"Good! I like the way you are sharing the top with Lita, Johnny."

Lita spun the top again, and Mary went to tell Brady he could come and play. Brady quickly found a wooden train with detachable cars, and he began pulling it around. Sally ran over. She had some cars from the train and wanted to attach them and play with the train, too. When Brady helped her put her cars on, Mary said, "Brady, I like the way you and Sally are sharing your toys with each other. Oh, look! Here's a caboose for your train, Brady. You can put it behind Sally's cars!"

Mary glanced at her watch, went to a cupboard, and came back with a book. "Who would like to hear a story?" she asked. Janet jumped up. "I would like to hear a story!" "Fine," said Mary, announcing to all of the children, "I am going to read a story." The children pulled chairs around in a circle and sat down.

Mary said, "Now let's see who can keep the rules. Remember what they are. First, we must be quiet and sit still during story time. Second, we raise our hands if we want to speak. Third, if we don't want to listen to the story, we go play quietly."

Mary began reading a story about a cat in a hat, and after a while Janet raised her hand; Mary called on her and she said, "I just got a cat and I named him The Cat in the Hat!" When the laughter died down, Mary said, "Janet remembered the rule; we always raise our hand if we want to speak during story time. Janet, you may help me turn the pages of the book." Mary continued reading to her engrossed audience.

Leah raised her hand, and Mary nodded. "When is the cat in the hat going home?" Mary smiled at Leah, reached over, and patted her shoulder warmly.

"That's a good question, Leah. Let's keep reading and we'll see."

When the cat in the hat had gone home and the story was over, Mary announced that it was time for juice and cookies.

"Yea! Yea!" shouted the children.

Mary kept their attention. "What do we do before juice and cookies? We pick up our toys, don't we!"

The children began putting things away, and Mary asked Randy to put away the blocks. He picked up some and, walking over to the box, dropped a few. He tried again, more carefully, and managed to get the blocks put away without dropping any more.

"You're doing a good job, Randy," said Mary. "You're working hard and being careful."

Juice and cookies were to be served in an adjoining room. The children went first to wash their hands. Mrs. Canessa accompanied Lita and the other girls, who chattered about the funny story and the thought of eating cookies. When they got to the table, the children sat down.

Mary noticed that Terry hadn't washed his hands and asked, "Terry, please wash your hands." When he returned, Mary let him help Sally pass out cookies, while Mary poured the juice. Mrs. Canessa noticed that although the children were eager for their cookies, they sat still. Sally seemed a little clumsy with her basket of cookies, but she managed to distribute them without dropping any. As Sally sat down, Mary said, "You did a good job, Sally. You didn't drop any, did you? Here's your juice."

The children chatted pleasantly while they munched their cookies. Mrs. Canessa was surprised that no one was throwing crumbs or spilling juice, or shouting back and forth. Since it was time for her to leave, she said goodbye to Lita and thanked Mary. As she walked out of the building, she thought about her visit. She had noticed that Mary often praised or smiled at the children when they were playing nicely or after they had performed a task. Mary did not yell at the children and did not discipline harshly, but the children behaved well and were happy there. Mrs. Canessa felt lucky that Lita was in Mary's class.

This book will help you understand why Mary is such a good teacher; and it will help you become a good teacher like her.

The children in Mary's class did not always behave the way they do today. Some children had been shy and withdrawn, others had been aggressive and uncooperative. Their behaviors were changed. The children were taught to behave the way they do today.

People are taught to behave the way they do.

In fact, most of the behaviors that we see people engaged in have been learned. Playing, talking, and working at tasks are all learned. Children can learn to be aggressive, and they can learn to be friendly. Children and adults learn from each other. Most of what we learn, we learn from other people.

People teach each other.

This is what psychologists mean when they speak of "social learning." When people learn, they change. When a child who does not share toys learns to share, he has changed. Two of society's most important functions— child rearing and education—are devoted to changing learners.

To learn is to change.

Once a visitor to Mary's class commented that he had never seen children who had learned to interact so well. What he overlooked was that he had never seen a teacher who had learned to change children like Mary.

Teachers are people who change learners.

But how do you best change learners? This travel guide is designed to answer that question.

How To Teach
How To Travel

Accelerating Consequences
Speeding Up

The single most important factor in learning a behavior is what happens immediately following the behavior. We will call what happens immediately following a behavior a *consequence*.

Here are some examples to give you practice in identifying *consequences:*

Terry pushes the peddle on a tricycle and the tricycle moves.

BEHAVIOR	pushes peddle
CONSEQUENCE	tricycle moves

Shawn builds a house of blocks and is praised by the teacher.

BEHAVIOR	builds house
CONSEQUENCE	praise

Bobby blows a toy trumpet and produces a loud sound.

BEHAVIOR	blows toy trumpet
CONSEQUENCE	loud sound

Johnny cries and is picked up by his mother.

BEHAVIOR	cries
CONSEQUENCE	picked up by mother

Exercise

Identify the *behavior* and the *immediate consequence* in the following examples.

Robert opens a book and sees a colorful picture.

BEHAVIOR	
CONSEQUENCE	

Susan moves her paint brush across the paper and leaves a pretty red line.

BEHAVIOR	
CONSEQUENCE	

Kara asks for a cookie and is given one by her mother.

BEHAVIOR	
CONSEQUENCE	

Jimmy turns a knob on the T.V. and a picture appears on the screen.

BEHAVIOR	
CONSEQUENCE	

If you identified Robert's *behavior* as opening a book, and the *consequence* that immediately followed as seeing a colorful picture, you were correct. Similarly, the pretty red line, a cookie, and a picture on the screen are the consequences that follow Susan's moving her paint brush, Kara's asking for a cookie, and Jimmy's turning a knob, respectively.

Exercise

Now write several of your own examples based upon the children you are with. Identify each behavior and its immediate consequence.

Examples:

BEHAVIOR	
CONSEQUENCE	

BEHAVIOR	
CONSEQUENCE	

BEHAVIOR	
CONSEQUENCE	

BEHAVIOR	
CONSEQUENCE	

Tell others what you are doing. Show this to them and see if they agree with you.

- In order to understand the effect of a consequence on a behavior, we need to know the *rate* at which the behavior occurs before we present a consequence. *Rate* includes (1) how many and (2) time.

To say that a child has shared eight times doesn't say much. To say that a child's *rate* of sharing is eight times an hour says a great deal. We measure behavior by the *rate* (behaviors per minute) of its occurrence, just as we measure speed by miles per hour.

There are two kinds of *consequences: accelerating* and *decelerating.* Parents and teachers have been using *accelerating* and *decelerating* consequences, referred to as rewards and punishments, for hundreds of years.

However, we are only now learning how to use consequences effectively to change children. One rule for using consequences effectively is that:

Consequences must immediately follow the behavior.

> Being quick
> does the trick.
> To delay
> doesn't pay.

What can we do if we want a behavior to speed up, that is, to increase in *rate?*

Maybe you noticed that Mary praised Johnny *immediately* after he shared his toy with Lita. Mary praised Johnny because Johnny needed to learn to share more, and Mary knew that behavior is affected by its *immediate consequences.* By consistently praising Johnny immediately after he shared his toy, Mary increased Johnny's *rate* of sharing during the first two weeks of school from two times during the six-hour school day to twelve times during the six-hour school day.

Behavior is affected by its immediate consequences.

JOHNNY	
BEHAVIOR	sharing
CONSEQUENCE	verbal praise
EFFECT ON BEHAVIOR	increase in RATE of sharing from 2 times/ 6 hours to 12 times/6 hours

By praising Johnny immediately following his sharing, Mary was able to increase Johnny's *rate* of sharing.

JOHNNY'S SHARING

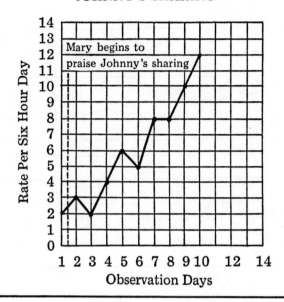

Rate Per Six Hour Day

Mary begins to praise Johnny's sharing

Observation Days

When a consequence immediately follows a behavior and the behavior then occurs more frequently, we call the consequence an *accelerating consequence*.

Because Johnny's *rate* of sharing increased, we can call praise an *accelerating consequence* for Johnny. Mary could not be sure that praise would be an *accelerating consequence* for Johnny until she used it and Johnny's *rate* of sharing increased. For Johnny, praise from Mary is an *accelerating consequence*. Mary can now confidently use praise to speed up many of Johnny's other behaviors.

If you wish to speed up a behavior,
present an
accelerating consequence
immediately following the behavior.

It would be a mistake to assume that a consequence such as teacher praise will be effective with all children.

When Leah asked a question, Mary smiled at Leah and touched her. Mary knows that smiling and touching are *accelerating consequences* for Leah. Mary used to verbally praise Leah but through careful observation

9

found that praise didn't work as an *accelerating consequence* for Leah. Mary then tried smiling and touching and found that they did work as *accelerating consequences.*

LEAH	
BEHAVIOR	question asking
CONSEQUENCE	verbal praise
EFFECT ON BEHAVIOR	no increase in rate of question asking

LEAH	
BEHAVIOR	question asking
CONSEQUENCE	smile and touch
EFFECT ON BEHAVIOR	increase in rate of question asking

Just because a consequence works as an accelerating consequence for one child does not necessarily mean that it will work as an accelerating consequence for another child.

You probably noticed that Mary used different consequences for Johnny and Leah. In order to speed up Johnny's rate of sharing, Mary praised him. In order to speed up Leah's rate of question asking, Mary smiled and touched her. Some consequences, like praise, smiling, and touching, usually work as accelerating consequences for most children. However, there are some consequences that may work as accelerating consequences for only one child, and some that may work as accelerating consequences for every child in your class but one!

It is important to remember that you must determine for each child what will work as an accelerating consequence. To identify what is an accelerating consequence for a particular child, you have to observe the child, and then present a consequence that you think may work following a behavior you wish to speed up. If the behavior speeds up, you have identified an accelerating consequence for the child.

Many parents and teachers have found that the following are accelerating consequences for most children.

Verbal Approval and Praise

"That's right."   "Groovy."   "You're a hard
"Good."   "Perfect."   worker."
"Great."   "Wow."   "You're getting
"Correct."   "Fantastic."   better."
"Excellent."   "I like that."   "I like the way
"Good thinking."   "You did a good job."   you're sharing."

Being Asked Questions

"What does that machine you made do?"
"How does that work?"
"How are you today?"
"Are you having a good time?"

Non-Verbal Approval

Smiling   Grinning
Nodding   Laughing
Clapping hands   Winking
Looking interested   Wrinkling nose

Physical Contact

Hugging   Holding
Touching   Shaking hands
Patting   Sitting on lap

Activities and Privileges

Going to the playground   Feeding animals
Playing with a new toy   Helping the teacher
Working on an art project   Passing out objects
Going on a field trip   Selecting a story to be
                                 read
                              Opportunity to engage in
                                 activity of own choice

Material Objects

Toys   Snacks
Trinkets   Art materials
Books   Games

When you present an accelerating consequence to a child, be enthusiastic. Show the child that you are really pleased with his behavior.

11

When you use praise as an accelerating consequence, direct the praise at a specific behavior such as, "I like the way you are paying attention," rather than using general statements such as, "You are a nice boy." Praise the *behavior*, not the total child. Always use *descriptive* praise that is clearly directed at a specific behavior.

Frequent "small" accelerating consequences are better than infrequent "big" accelerating consequences.

Social consequences such as praise, approval, and physical contact are always available, don't cost anything, are easy to present, and are effective as accelerating consequences for most children.

Some children are not very responsive to social consequences presented by adults, such as praise, approval, and physical contact. With these children, you may find it necessary to use powerful accelerating consequences such as material objects. If you do use material objects as accelerating consequences always praise the child as you are presenting the object. By using this procedure, praise will soon start to work as an accelerating consequence. Then you can begin to gradually substitute social consequences for material consequences.

Caution: Don't use accelerating consequences that are more powerful than necessary to speed up the child's behavior. If praise works, don't use candy!

You get what you give! If you present accelerating consequences to others, they are more likely to present accelerating consequences to you.

In addition to using accelerating consequences with an individual child, you can also use them with a group of children. Often you can speed up a specific behavior of all of the children in a group, such as listening or playing together, by presenting the group with an accelerating consequence. For example, you may verbally praise the group, "You are all playing together nicely;" or present an activity to the group, "You all listened so well that I have a special treat for you—here is a new game that we can all play;" or present a privilege to the group, "You sure know how to play together well. I need children who play together well to help me set out the art materials for the class." Everything you have learned about using accelerating consequences with an individual child also applies to using accelerating consequences with a group of children.

Children can accelerate behavior too!

Mary overhears Annie saying to Gerald, "You really did a fine job tying your shoes." Mary immediately smiles at Annie and makes a point of telling her what a good helper she is.

Mary is a skillful teacher and skillful teachers soon have many helpers. Here is an example of how Mary develops helpers.

To begin, Mary presents accelerating consequences directly to a child, "You really did a fine job tying your shoes, Gerald." Next, Mary brings one of the child's peers into the interaction, "Gerald did a really fine job tying his shoes, didn't he, Annie?" Annie gets Mary's attention for being her "helper" in presenting Gerald with an accelerating consequence; and Gerald gets the approval of one of his peers in addition to the approval of Mary. Later, Annie congratulates Gerald for his shoe tying, without any prompting from Mary, and Mary is quick to praise Annie for being her "helper."

Activities as Accelerating Consequences

Skillful teachers have also learned that the opportunity to engage in a "preferred" activity can serve as a powerful accelerating consequence for other behaviors. There are several advantages to using preferred activities as accelerating consequences, not the least of which is that the opportunity to employ them is always available. Another important advantage is that it is relatively easy to identify those activities which will act as accelerating consequences—they are the activities that the children frequently engage in when they are allowed to choose what they will do.

Many teachers use this principle by arranging a child's activities so that the child is required to engage in a less preferred activity in order to engage in a highly preferred activity. For example, "Tommy, *if* you pick up the blocks, *then* you can go outside and play." "Jane, *if* you and Ron play together cooperatively until snack time, *then* both of you can help me pass out cookies." *If–then* statements are frequently used by good teachers.

For children to learn a new behavior, there must be immediate accelerating consequences presented following the behavior. At first, these accelerating consequences must be *consistently* presented every time the behavior occurs. Thus, when Janet is just beginning to learn how to share,

Mary praises her *every time* the behavior occurs. Mary has previously determined that praise is an accelerating consequence for Janet.

If you wish to speed up a behavior
that is just being learned,
consistently present an
accelerating consequence
immediately following the behavior
every time the behavior occurs.

Do not expect to see an immediate change in a behavior following the presentation of a single accelerating consequence. Behaviors usually change slowly, and the effect upon a behavior of presenting a single accelerating consequence following the behavior is small. In order to successfully change a behavior, it is necessary, therefore, to present over a period of time, many accelerating consequences immediately following the behavior.

For example, if a child is just beginning to learn how to take turns, the teacher may present an accelerating consequence such as praise *every time* the behavior occurs. Later, after the behavior is more established, the teacher can begin to praise the child's taking turns less often—maybe initially every other time the child takes turns and later, every fifth time. However, if a teacher stops consistently praising the child's behavior too abruptly, the child may stop taking turns. If this begins to happen, the teacher must again praise the behavior every time it occurs. By slowly increasing the number of times that the child must take turns before he is praised, the teacher will, in time, be able to maintain the child's taking turns at a high rate, even though the child is only occasionally praised for the behavior.

In fact, studies have shown that once a behavior is learned, it is more likely to be maintained if it is only occasionally followed by accelerating consequences.

If you wish to maintain a behavior
that is already learned,
occasionally present an
accelerating consequence
immediately following the behavior.

Things that are taken for granted often go away.

Caution: Do not take desirable behavior for granted; be sure to occasionally follow it with an accelerating consequence. Try to

"catch the child being good" and present an accelerating consequence immediately following the behavior.

Caution: Accelerating consequences that are overused often
lose their effectiveness. If a teacher frequently uses the same accelerating consequences such as, "Wow, that's great," it may become
less and less effective. Remember to always vary the accelerating
consequences that you use. Children like variety, too.

You have just learned how to speed up behavior, and you are
about to learn how to slow down behavior. Most of your efforts as a
teacher should be directed towards speeding up desirable behaviors
rather than towards slowing down undesirable behaviors. Focus most
of your attention upon the desirable behaviors the children are dis-
playing. Look for behaviors to speed up in each and every child.

Caution: Make sure that all children are presented with
accelerating consequences. Do not neglect a child or "play favorites."

Eliminating Accelerating Consequences
Slowing Down

Children are neither good nor bad. Rather, they have learned some
behaviors that we call good and some that we call bad. When a child has
learned undesirable behaviors, we must change them for the benefit of the
child.

You may recall that Robert whined when the tower of blocks he was
building fell over. Mary had been carefully observing Robert for a few days,
and had found that he whined an average of eight times an hour and that
she had occasionally gone over to him while he was whining to see what
was wrong. Mary wanted to decrease Robert's rate of whining. She knew
that her attention was an accelerating consequence for Robert and realized
that her attending to him when he whined was probably maintaining his
whining.

ROBERT	
BEHAVIOR	whining
CONSEQUENCE	attention from Mary
EFFECT ON BEHAVIOR	possibly maintains whining at a rate of 8 times an hour

For the rest of the week Mary *ignored* Robert whenever he was whining. By the end of the week, Robert's rate of whining dropped to less than one time an hour.

ROBERT	
BEHAVIOR	whining
CONSEQUENCE	ignored by Mary
EFFECT ON BEHAVIOR	decrease in rate of whining from 8 times an hour to less than 1 time an hour

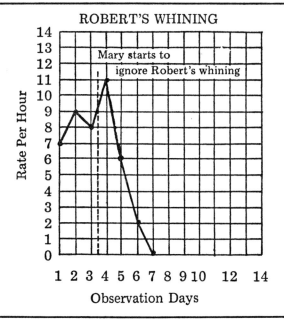

ROBERT'S WHINING

Mary starts to ignore Robert's whining

Rate Per Hour

Observation Days

By eliminating the accelerating consequence—attention—which was maintaining Robert's whining, Mary was able to decrease the rate of Robert's whining.

If you wish to slow down a behavior,
eliminate the
accelerating consequence
that is maintaining the behavior.

16

For long-term results the most effective means of slowing down a behavior is to eliminate the accelerating consequence that is maintaining the behavior. Provided you are consistent and do not occasionally present an accelerating consequence following the undesirable behavior, the undesirable behavior will slowly but surely slow down, just as if you took your foot off the accelerator while your car was moving.

Caution: Don't expect a behavior to immediately decrease in rate when you start to ignore it. Sometimes the behavior will increase in rate before it begins to decrease (see example on page 16).

Once a behavior stops "paying off," it will start going away.

Caution: If you do not *consistently ignore* an undesirable behavior, it will not slow down. By occasionally attending to the undesirable behavior, you may maintain it at a high rate. Recall that once a behavior is learned, it is more likely to be maintained if it is only occasionally followed by accelerating consequences.

When an undesirable behavior occurs, look for the accelerating consequence that is maintaining it. It may be your own behavior.

Caution: Desirable behaviors will also slow down if they are *ignored.* Do not make the mistake of accidentally slowing down a behavior you do not want to slow down. Always remember to present accelerating consequences following desirable behaviors and to eliminate accelerating consequences *(ignore)* following undesirable behaviors.

Exercise

Select a behavior of one of the children you are with that you would like to slow down. Consistently *ignore* the behavior whenever it occurs. The behavior I would like to slow down is: _____
_____
_____

Eliminating All Accelerating Consequences
Slowing Down

Social Isolation

You now know how to gradually slow down behavior. Sometimes, however, gradually slowing down is not enough. You need to stop! In these situations, you must use your brakes.

If Brady hits other children and takes their toys, you cannot just ignore Brady and wait for his rate of hitting to slowly decrease. In fact, if you were to try this, you would most likely find that his rate of hitting would not decrease at all. The accelerating consequences that maintain Brady's hitting are, most likely, the submission of his victim, peer attention, and getting the victim's toy.

During the first day of school, Mary observed that Brady hit approximately two times an hour.

BRADY	
BEHAVIOR	hitting and taking toys
CONSEQUENCE	submission of victim, peer attention, getting the victim's toy
EFFECT ON BEHAVIOR	maintains hitting and taking toys at a rate of 2 times an hour

Mary must use a procedure which will quickly slow down Brady's rate of hitting and taking toys. Since there are a large number of accelerating consequences which, most likely, maintain Brady's hitting and taking toys, Mary decides to use a procedure which will eliminate all accelerating consequences for Brady's undesirable behavior.

The next time Brady hits another child, Mary immediately tells him to go sit by himself far away from any other children. After two to three minutes, Mary tells Brady that he can return to the group and play with the other children as long as he plays nicely. Mary continues to consistently use this procedure every time Brady hits another child or takes another child's toy, and she finds that after three days this behavior no longer occurs.

18

BRADY	
BEHAVIOR	hitting and taking toys
CONSEQUENCE	social isolation
EFFECT ON BEHAVIOR	rate of hitting and taking toys decreases from 2 times an hour to 0

BRADY'S HITTING

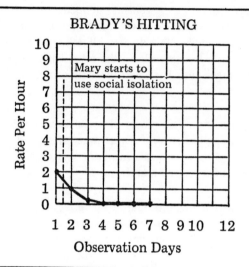

By placing Brady in social isolation immediately following his hitting, Mary was able to decrease Brady's rate of hitting.

If you wish to quickly slow down a behavior,
use **social isolation** to eliminate
all accelerating consequences
for a short period of time.

The effectiveness of social isolation as a procedure for quickly slowing down a behavior depends on really eliminating all accelerating consequences. If Brady could play with an attractive toy or communicate with another child while he was removed from the group, Mary would not have eliminated all accelerating consequences. If all accelerating consequences are not eliminated, the behavior will not slow down. Also, if a child cries or throws a tantrum when he is removed from the group, he should be ignored as long as this behavior

19

continues. He should be invited to return to the group only when he is sitting quietly.

Select a location to be used for social isolation that is both isolated and dull.

When Mary places a child in social isolation, she tells the child in a firm, calm, matter-of-fact way why he is being removed from the group. She does not use general statements such as, "You were a bad boy." Instead, she describes the behavior that is causing the problem, for example, "We do not hit other people here. You hit Robert, so you will have to leave the other children and sit on this chair. Stay seated until I tell you that you can get up." *Be descriptive.*

Caution: The effectiveness of social isolation depends partly on its rarity. The less it is used, the more effective it will be. Also, the duration of time that a child is in social isolation should be relatively short (i.e., 2 to 3 minutes).

In order for this procedure to be effective, the situation that the child is removed from must contain accelerating consequences. If a child is in a situation that does not contain any accelerating consequences, you cannot use this procedure to slow down the child's behavior since there are no accelerating consequences to eliminate. In fact, if the child is in a situation that is aversive, such as an unpleasant classroom that he does not like, and you remove him from this unpleasant situation whenever he displays an undesirable behavior, the rate of his undesirable behavior will increase. This is because you are, in effect, allowing the child to escape from the unpleasant situation whenever he displays an undesirable behavior.

The frequency of behavior problems is often a function of what is happening in the classroom in general. Undesirable behavior is more likely to occur during some activities and some settings than in others. For example, a child who hits is often more likely to hit another child during group participation activities when all of the children are close together, than during activities where they are separated; and such aggression is typically more common in hallways and playgrounds than in the classroom. In these cases it may be possible to reduce the undesirable behavior by controlling the activities in which a child participates. Undesirable behaviors are also more likely when children are bored or placed in a failure situation. If this is the case, the undesirable behavior can often be greatly reduced by arranging learning activities that allow the children to succeed.

Decelerating Consequences
Slowing Down

Just as there are consequences that speed up or accelerate behavior, there are also consequences that slow down or decelerate behavior. When a consequence immediately follows a behavior and the behavior then occurs less frequently, we call the consequence a *decelerating consequence*.

The presentation of a decelerating consequence immediately following a behavior is commonly referred to as punishment. There are certain situations that may require the presentation of a decelerating consequence. Mary prefers not to use decelerating consequences for the following reasons:

1. Experiments have clearly shown that it is much more effective to teach a child to perform desirable behaviors by immediately presenting accelerating consequences following the desirable behavior than to punish the child for an undesirable behavior.

2. Children and adults often learn to dislike people who punish them, activities in which they are punished, and places where they are punished. This is reflected in statements such as:
   "I don't like my teacher."
   "I hate arithmetic."
   "I don't want to go to school."
   It is also reflected in such behaviors as lying, cheating, truancy, doing things behind one's back, etc.

3. Children and adults often learn to escape from or avoid people, activities, or places associated with the use of punishment. When children begin to escape from and avoid the adults who are attempting to socialize and teach them, the adults may lose the opportunity to continue to influence the child.

21

4. Punishment may cause a child to become anxious. Most adults are familiar with the symptoms of anxiety— muscle tension, upset stomach, increase in respiration and blood pressure, "nervousness"— and they recognize that anxiety may interfere with many behaviors. Not everyone understands, however, that anxiety can be the result of punishment. If a child is often punished by a teacher or parent in the class or in the home, just being around the individuals who punished him or the location where he was punished may cause the child to feel anxious. An anxious child will be neither happy or productive, nor will he learn well.

5. Teachers or parents who use punishment to change a child may lose their effectiveness in presenting accelerating consequences to the child. Verbal praise and approval and physical contact such as touching and hugging presented to a child by an adult may not be as effective as accelerating consequences if the same adult frequently scolds or spanks the child.

6. If physical punishment such as slapping or spanking are used on a child by an adult, the child may imitate this aggressive behavior. That is, children often do what they observe adults doing. We might expect, therefore, that children of parents who are aggressive towards them would be more aggressive towards other children.

7. Punishment is just not a very effective means of slowing down a behavior in the long run. Unless the undesirable behavior is punished every time it occurs and the punishment is extremely severe, the undesirable behavior will continue to occur. Since it is difficult to always be there to punish an undesirable behavior every time it occurs and since the use of an extremely severe punishment would likely cause more problems—emotional reactions such as anxiety and fear—than it would cure, punishment is not a practical means of changing a child.

8. If a behavior is punished and then the use of punishment is discontinued, or if the person who delivers the punishment is absent, then the punished behavior will speed up, often to a higher rate than before punishment.

9. Punishments that are used over a period of time tend to lose their effectiveness. The practical effect is that a child who is punished frequently tends to become immune to the punishment. To get the

same effect in decelerating the punished behavior, the person delivering the punishments must continuously increase the severity of the punishments making them harsher and harsher.

10. When parents or teachers punish the undesirable behavior of a child, the undesirable behavior will immediately decrease in rate, only to later increase in rate. However, the initial decrease in the rate of the child's undesirable behavior often works as an accelerating consequence for the parents' or teachers' punishing behavior. This leads to an increase in the use of punishment by the parents and teachers since punishment seems to be an effective means of slowing down an undesirable behavior, although it really is not effective in the long run. In this manner, parents and teachers can learn to rely on coercion, threats, and punishment to influence behavior.

11. Psychologists have found that in social interactions individuals "get what they give." Those individuals who present accelerating consequences to others also receive accelerating consequences from others. Likewise, the more decelerating consequences an individual presents to others, the more decelerating consequences he will receive from others.

Given all of these reasons for not punishing a child, it is easy to understand why Mary is extremely reluctant to use decelerating consequences. However, there are rare circumstances in which Mary may find it necessary to do so. For example, if Mary decides that she cannot allow a child to continue to behave in a certain manner because of the risk of injury to himself or to others and all other means of slowing down this dangerous behavior have failed, she will wait for the behavior to occur and immediately present what she hopes will be a decelerating consequence. This may be a reprimand such as "stop," "no," or "sit down." Such a reprimand will be effective for some children in slowing down the dangerous behavior. However, teachers often make the mistake of assuming that a reprimand such as "stop," "no," or "sit down" will always work as a decelerating consequence. This is not true. Psychologists have found that the more often teachers tell some children to "sit down," the more often they "stand up." The only way to know if a reprimand is a decelerating consequence for an individual child is to present the reprimand and observe whether the rate of the behavior that it immediately follows slows down, stays the same, or speeds up. If the rate of the behavior slows down, then we know that the reprimand is a decelerating consequence for that particular child.

As a final resort, if all other means of changing the dangerous behavior of a child have not succeeded, Mary may have to consistently present a stronger decelerating consequence to the child immediately following the behavior every time the behavior occurs.

> If you wish to immediately slow down a behavior
> that is dangerous to the child or to others,
> consistently present a
> **decelerating consequence**
> immediately following the behavior
> **every time**
> the behavior occurs.

Before Mary presents a decelerating consequence, she always gives the child a warning. Then if the behavior continues, she will present in a firm, calm, matter-of-fact way what she hopes will be a decelerating consequence immediately following the behavior. While Mary is presenting the decelerating consequence, she explains to the child in a descriptive manner what behavior is being punished. For many children the warning alone will work or will come to work as a decelerating consequence.

The warning is basically a "threat" that if the undesirable behavior continues, then a decelerating consequence will be presented. The warning should be specific; it should tell the child what behavior is to be stopped and what decelerating consequence will be presented if the behavior occurs again. When giving a warning, be certain that you are willing and able to carry out the implied threat if the undesirable behavior does occur.

You now know how to speed up a behavior:

> If you wish to speed up a behavior
> that is just being learned,
> **consistently** present an
> accelerating consequence
> immediately following the behavior
> **every time** the behavior occurs.

If you wish to maintain a behavior
that is already learned,
occasionally present an
accelerating consequence
. immediately following the behavior.

You now also know how to slow down a behavior:

If you wish to slow down a behavior,
eliminate the
accelerating consequence
that is maintaining the behavior.

If you wish to quickly slow down a behavior,
use **social isolation** to eliminate all
accelerating consequences
for a short period of time.

If you wish to immediately slow down a behavior
that is dangerous to the child or to others,
consistently present a
decelerating consequence
immediately following the behavior
every time the behavior occurs.

One of the most powerful means yet discovered to change a learner
is to:
1. Slow down undesirable behaviors, and
2. At the same time, speed up desirable behaviors that are incompatible
   with the undesirable behaviors.

For example, you recall that Mary found it necessary to slow down
Brady's hitting and taking toys from other children. To slow down this
behavior Mary made Brady leave the children he was playing with and sit
by himself far away from any other children whenever he hit a child or
took his toy. At the same time Mary was careful to speed up Brady's asking for toys, cooperating, and sharing by immediately presenting an accelerating consequence, praise, whenever any of these behaviors occurred.
Mary did this for two reasons:

1. Asking for toys, cooperating, and sharing are incompatible with hitting and taking toys. This is easy to understand. If a child is cooperating, he can't be hitting. One way of slowing down hitting, therefore is to speed up cooperating.
2. Asking for toys, cooperating, and sharing are desirable behaviors that Mary wants to teach Brady.

Whenever you slow down an undesirable behavior, at the same time speed up desirable behaviors that are incompatible with the undesirable behavior. You can accomplish this with most children by simply *ignoring* those behaviors that you would like to slow down and *praising* competing behaviors that you would like to speed up.

The most effective way to prevent undesirable behavior is to arrange conditions which produce desirable behavior.

Exercise

Listed below are a number of undesirable behaviors. Find a desirable behavior that is incompatible with each undesirable behavior.

Undesirable behaviors	Incompatible desirable behaviors
1. Whining	1. _____
2. Yelling	2. _____
3. Grabbing another child's toy	3. _____ _____
4. Interrupting while another person is speaking	4. _____ _____ _____
5. Going out of turn	5. _____
6. Spilling juice	6. _____
7. Verbally threatening another child	7. _____ _____

Tell others what you are doing. Show this to them and see if they agree with you.

Shaping
Starting
If a child is not capable of performing these pro-social behaviors because they are not in his repertoire, then it will be necessary to teach the

child these behaviors. This requires the development or selection of an instructional program to teach pro-social behaviors. This may involve *shaping* the behavior.

One of the children in Mary's class is named Eric. When Eric entered Mary's class, he had never played with other children before. During Eric's first two days at school, he isolated himself and played with a simple toy in a repetitive manner or ran around the room disturbing other children. By observing Eric for these first two days, Mary found that he did not play with the other children at all. Mary wants all of the children in her class to play together. However, since Eric never played with other children, Mary could not simply speed up his playing with other children by presenting accelerating consequences following the behavior. Mary must therefore design an individualized program to teach Eric to play with other children. Mary knows that there are many steps involved in learning to play with other children and that when we teach any new behavior we must start where the child currently is and *shape* the new behavior in a single step at a time.

For Eric the first step is to play quietly by himself. For the first two days of the program Mary consistently comes over and talks with Eric when he is playing quietly by himself. By the end of the second day Mary observes that Eric no longer runs around the room and is spending most of his time playing quietly by himself.

ERIC	
BEHAVIOR	running around the room
CONSEQUENCE	ignored by Mary
EFFECT ON BEHAVIOR	decrease in behavior
BEHAVIOR	playing quietly by himself
CONSEQUENCE	attention from Mary
EFFECT ON BEHAVIOR	increase in behavior

The next step for Eric is to play quietly by himself near other children. During the third day of the program, Mary only attends to Eric when he is playing quietly by himself near other children. By the afternoon Eric plays only near other children.

ERIC	
BEHAVIOR	playing quietly by himself
CONSEQUENCE	ignored by Mary
EFFECT ON BEHAVIOR	decrease in behavior
BEHAVIOR	playing quietly by himself near other children
CONSEQUENCE	attention from Mary
EFFECT ON BEHAVIOR	increase in behavior

The next day Mary causes Eric to take another step by presenting him with accelerating consequences only when he is playing together with other children.

After several days of attending to and praising Eric when he is playing together with other children, Mary observes that Eric now spends most of his time in school playing together with other children.

ERIC	
BEHAVIOR	playing quietly alone near other children
CONSEQUENCE	ignored by Mary
EFFECT ON BEHAVIOR	decrease in behavior
BEHAVIOR	playing with other children
CONSEQUENCE	attention and verbal praise from Mary
EFFECT ON BEHAVIOR	increase in behavior

Learning should be divided into small steps.

To teach a new behavior by *shaping:*

1. Determine where the child's behavior currently is.

2. Decide what you want to teach the child, that is, where you want the behavior to go (destination).

3. Break the learning down into small steps that start where the child's behavior currently is and move toward where you want the child's behavior to go (destination).

4. Present accelerating consequences immediately following each behavior that is a step closer to the destination.

5. Present accelerating consequences only for those behaviors that are closer and closer to the destination.

6. Continue to raise the criterion for the presentation of accelerating consequences until you reach the destination.

It is important to recognize that most complex behaviors are slowly learned as a series of small steps. To learn effectively, the child must be presented with accelerating consequences following each step in the right direction.

Exercise

Go back and reread pages 26-28. Note how each of the above principles is used.

Caution: Present accelerating consequences following only those behaviors that are "closer and closer" to the destination. If you were to continue to present accelerating consequences following the early steps, the child would not move on to the next step. On the other hand, if you try to move too fast and take steps that are too large, you will slow down the behavior if the criterion for the presentation of accelerating consequences is not met.

Exercise

Select a new behavior that you would like to teach to a child. Be specific.

The behavior is: _____

_____

Now break this behavior down into several small steps:

Step 1. _____

Step 2. _____

Step 3. _____

Step 4. _____

Step 5. _____

Try shaping the new behavior.

The next section describes how to start behaviors using *cues*. In general it is much more efficient to start most new behaviors by using *cues* rather than by *shaping* the behavior. As a rule, therefore, you should try to start new behaviors using *cues* and use *shaping* only if that doesn't work.

Cues and Modeling
Starting

Earlier we said that the single most important factor in learning a behavior is what happens following a behavior. We found that by using consequences effectively we could speed up and slow down behaviors.

Now we are going to look at what happens before a behavior occurs. Mary enters the room with a storybook and says, "Who would like to hear a story?" Janet answers, "I would like to hear a story," and Mary begins reading to her.

JANET	
BEHAVIOR	asking to hear a story
CONSEQUENCE	hearing a story read
EFFECT ON BEHAVIOR	unspecified

Janet's saying, "I would like to hear a story," was preceded by Mary's saying, "Who would like to hear a story?" We will call the event which happens immediately before a behavior a *cue*.

JANET	
CUE	Mary's asking who would like to hear a story
BEHAVIOR	asking to hear a story
CONSEQUENCE	hearing a story read
EFFECT ON BEHAVIOR	unspecified

Here are some more examples of *cues:*

David sees a jack-in-the-box in the play room. He picks it up and pushes a button on it, and a little clown pops up out of the door.

DAVID	
CUE	sees jack-in-the box
BEHAVIOR	picks it up and pushes a button
CONSEQUENCE	little clown pops up
EFFECT ON BEHAVIOR	unspecified

Mary sets out paper and paints on a table. Betty and Mark come over to the table and begin painting. Mary comments about what a nice job they are doing. Betty and Mark continue painting.

BETTY & MARK	
CUE	paper and paints on a table
BEHAVIOR	painting
CONSEQUENCE	verbal praise from Mary
EFFECT ON BEHAVIOR	behavior continues

Ann sees a group of children jumping rope. She runs up and asks if she can play too, and then gets a turn jumping rope.

ANN	
CUE	children jumping rope
BEHAVIOR	asks to play
CONSEQUENCE	turn jumping rope
EFFECT ON BEHAVIOR	unspecified

Exercise

Identify the *cue, behavior,* and *immediate consequence* in the following examples.

Roberta sees a napkin on the floor, picks it up, and throws it away. Mary says to Roberta, "My, you're neat."

ROBERTA	
CUE	
BEHAVIOR	
CONSEQUENCE	
EFFECT ON BEHAVIOR	unspecified

Mary tells Carol to "sit quietly," and when she is sitting quietly, Mary reads a story to her.

CAROL	
CUE	
BEHAVIOR	
CONSEQUENCE	
EFFECT ON BEHAVIOR	unspecified

Chris sees a piece of candy on a table. He picks it up and puts it in his mouth.

CHRIS	
CUE	
BEHAVIOR	
CONSEQUENCE	
EFFECT ON BEHAVIOR	unspecified

Mary says, "John, please help me carry this tray." John carries the tray to the kitchen and is told, "Thank you."

JOHN	
CUE	
BEHAVIOR	
CONSEQUENCE	
EFFECT ON BEHAVIOR	unspecified

If you identified the *cue* in the first example as the napkin on the floor, the *behavior* as picking up the napkin and throwing it away, and the *immediate consequence* as Mary saying, "My, you're neat," you were correct.

You were also correct if you identified the *cues* in the other examples as: Mary's telling Carol to "sit quietly," Chris's seeing a piece of candy, and Mary's saying "John, please help me carry this tray."

Behaviors in the other examples as: sitting quietly, picking up candy and putting it in the mouth, and carrying the tray.

Consequences in the other examples as: being read a story, having candy in the mouth, and being told "Thank you."

Exercise

Now write your own examples based upon the children you are with. Identify the *cue, behavior, immediate consequences,* and *effect on behavior* if known.

Example:

CUE	
BEHAVIOR	
CONSEQUENCE	
EFFECT ON BEHAVIOR	

Example:

CUE	
BEHAVIOR	
CONSEQUENCE	
EFFECT ON BEHAVIOR	

Tell others what you are doing. Show this to them and see if they agree with you.

Cues are used to start behaviors.

Often we can identify what the cues are for certain behaviors. If we can identify the cues, then we can initiate or start a behavior by presenting the appropriate cue.

For example, Mary would like Terry to wash his hands before he eats. She decides not to wait until Terry washes his hands on his own. Instead she presents a *cue:* "Terry, please wash your hands." Terry washes his hands, and Mary lets him help pass out cookies to the other children.

TERRY	
CUE	"Terry please wash your hands."
BEHAVIOR	washes hands
CONSEQUENCE	helps pass out cookies
EFFECT ON BEHAVIOR	unspecified

Of course, if we want the behavior to speed up, we must immediately follow the occurrence of the behavior with an accelerating consequence.

As all teachers know, one of the most effective *cues* is the behavior of other children and adults.

People often behave like other people they see.

Psychologists refer to this as *imitation.* Studies have shown that both children and adults learn many behaviors by imitating a model. Similarly, studies have shown that children are more likely to imitate others who have prestige and who control the consequences they receive. Because of this, effective teachers are always careful in the way they behave since they know that children often behave as they behave. Teachers can make use of this as an effective means of teaching by behaving the way they want students to behave. Teachers should always model the behavior they are trying to develop. If learners are to be enthusiastic, you should be enthusiastic; if they are to display empathy, so should you.

Studies have also demonstrated that children will tend to imitate other children and engage in the activities other children are participating in when they see or have seen the other children receive accelerating consequences. Good teachers often make use of this by prompting a desired behavior for a particular child by presenting an accelerating consequence to another "model" child who is exhibiting the desirable behavior. For example, if during story time Sam is attending to the story and James is not, the teacher can make a point of telling Sam how well he is listening.

Upon observing this, James is likely to begin attending and the teacher can then comment on how well he is listening. Thus, a child's undesirable behavior can be slowed down and a desirable behavior speeded up without any direct reference to the fact that the child was engaging in an undesirable behavior.

Exercise

Select and teach a child a new behavior that you think the child could learn by imitation.
The behavior is: _____

_____

Say to the child, "Watch me and do as I do," then model the behavior. If the child imitates the behavior, immediately present an accelerating consequence.

A common *cue* used by many teachers is the stating of a rule. If you want to establish rules, you should:

● State the rule in a positive manner. A rule should tell the child how he is to behave, not suggest ways of misbehaving.

● Keep the rule short, specific, and to the point.

● State rules that are easy to understand and enforce.

● Limit the number of rules to three or four. Psychologists have found that a small number of rules works better than a large number.

● Be consistent in the application of the rules.

● Always accelerate behaviors that "follow the rules." A rule is only important to the child if it tells him how to behave in order to receive accelerating consequences.

● Use the children that are "following the rule" as models by presenting them with accelerating consequences and announcing to the class why they are receiving the accelerating consequences. ("Janet remembered the rule; we always raise our hand if we want to speak during story time; Janet you can help me turn the pages of the book.")

● Gradually reduce the number of times that you state the rule and continue to accelerate behaviors that "follow the rule." Try to reach the point where you are maintaining the behavior without having to state the rule.

Consistency
Traveling Smoothly

The secret to traveling smoothly is to be *consistent* and to *consistently* apply the principles presented in this chapter.

It would be a mistake to think that these principles are used in isolation. In fact, the opposite is true; effective teachers may be using several of the principles simultaneously. As an example, to prevent and deal with aggression in a classroom an effective teacher would:

Present accelerating consequences for pro-social behavior,

Model pro-social behavior,

Teach pro-social behavior such as interaction skills (sharing, taking turns, cooperating, negotiating, etc.),

Ignore minor aggression if the behavior would be accelerated by teacher attention accompanying any intervention, and present accelerating consequences in an obvious manner to other children who are engaged in appropriate behaviors.

If the aggressive behavior continues, interrupt it as early in the chain as possible,

Structure the situation by arranging carefully the activities and the grouping of children,

If aggressive behavior still continues, eliminate all accelerating consequences when aggression occurs,

As a last resort in extreme cases, present decelerating consequences to immediately decrease the aggressive behavior.

Summary of Chapter One

1. Behavior is influenced most by its *immediate consequence.*

2. There are two kinds of *consequences: accelerating* and *decelerating.*

3. *Consequences* must *immediately* follow the behavior.

4. Behavior is measured by its *rate* of occurrence. *Rate* includes how many and time.

5. An *accelerating consequence* increases the rate of the behavior it immediately follows.

6. If you wish to speed up a behavior that is just being learned, *consistently* present an accelerating consequence immediately following the behavior *every time* the behavior occurs.

7. If you wish to maintain a behavior that is already learned, *occasionally* present an accelerating consequence immediately following the behavior.

8. If you wish to slow down a behavior, *eliminate* the accelerating consequence that is maintaining the behavior.

9. If you wish to quickly slow down a behavior, use *social isolation* to eliminate all accelerating consequences for a short period of time. Social isolation works best if it is seldom used.

10. *A decelerating consequence* decreases the rate of the behavior it immediately follows.

11. The presentation of a decelerating consequence immediately following a behavior is referred to as *punishment*. There are a large number of reasons for not using *punishment*.

12. If you wish to immediately slow down a behavior that is dangerous to the child or to others, consistently present a *decelerating consequence* immediately following the behavior *every time* the behavior occurs.

13. One of the most powerful means yet discovered to change a learner is to:
    A. Slow down undesirable behaviors, and
    B. At the same time speed up desirable behaviors that are incompatible with the undesirable behaviors.

14. To teach a new behavior by *shaping:*
   A. Determine where the child's behavior currently is,
   B. Decide what you want to teach the child, that is, where you want the behavior to go (destination),
   C. Break the learning down into small steps that start where the child's behavior currently is and move toward where you want the child's behavior to go,
   D. Present accelerating consequences immediately following each behavior that is a step closer to the destination,
   E. Only present accelerating consequences for those behaviors that are closer and closer to the destination,
   F. Continue to raise the criterion for the presentation of accelerating consequences until you reach the destination.
15. An event occurring immediately before a behavior is called a *cue.*

16. *Cues* are used to start behaviors.

17. After a cue starts an appropriate behavior, immediately follow the behavior with an accelerating consequence.

18. People often behave like other people they see.

19. *Be consistent* and *consistently* apply these principles.

What To Teach
Where To Go

2

Need for Objectives
Selecting Destinations

Now that you know how to travel, you are ready to learn the most important travel skill: *deciding where to go.* Knowing how to travel is of little help to anyone if they don't know where they want to go.

Mary always knows where she wants to go with each child. One of the reasons she is so effective as a teacher is that she knows what she wants to teach. Johnny didn't learn to share and Leah didn't learn to ask questions until Mary decided to teach them these skills. Mary selected a destination to move these children toward— she had an objective.

> If you don't have an objective, you don't know where you want to go. If you don't know where you want to go, you probably will not get to a place you would like to be.

In selecting objectives for a particular child, you are asking the question, "What does this child need to learn that I can teach him?"

To answer this question, you may find it useful to compare the child to other children his own age. This comparison may suggest several behaviors that the child needs to learn. You might also consider the behaviors that the child needs in order to get along more effectively in his current environment, and in the environments he will later be entering. Finally, you may wish to think about and specify those behaviors that you consider to be desirable in a child.

41

If you like it and the child needs it, select it as an objective.

Good objectives are good for the child and good for you.

Defining Objectives
Specifying A Destination

Whenever Mary selects an objective, she knows from experience that for the objective to be useful to her in teaching, she must *specify* the objective clearly and in detail.

Mary has found a simple way to do this by asking herself three questions:

What *behavior* do I want the learner to perform?

In what *setting* do I want the behavior to occur?

How well, or to what *criterion*, do I want the behavior to be performed?

Here is how it works. Mary selects an objective: she decides to teach Sally to pass out cookies. After drawing and labeling the box below, Mary asks herself the first question.

SALLY
SETTING:
BEHAVIOR:
CRITERION:

What *behavior* do I want Sally to perform?

SALLY
SETTING:
BEHAVIOR: pass out a cookie to each child seated at the table
CRITERION:

(Is this enough? *No!* Mary doesn't want Sally passing out cookies during story time or free play. Mary must specify the *setting* in which the behavior is to occur. So she asks—)

In what *setting* do I want the behavior to occur?

SALLY	
SETTING:	During juice and cookie time when all of the children are seated at the table, Sally is to
BEHAVIOR:	pass out a cookie to each child seated at the table
CRITERION:	

(Is this enough? *No!* Mary doesn't want Sally to take fifteen minutes to perform the task or to drop the cookies on the floor. Mary must specify how well, or to what *criterion,* Sally should perform the task. So she asks—)

How well, or to what *criterion,* do I want the behavior to be performed?

SALLY	
SETTING:	During juice and cookie time when all of the children are seated at the table, Sally is to
BEHAVIOR:	pass out a cookie to each child seated at the table
CRITERION:	within 3 minutes of when she starts, without dropping any of the cookies, walking, either silently or talking in a moderate voice.

Now Mary has specified the objective clearly and in detail. Mary will know when Sally has reached this destination. In fact, she has specified the objective so well that a stranger could walk into her class, be given the objective she specified, and be able to determine if Sally has reached the objective. This is known as the *stranger test.*

43

Stranger Test

If you give the objective you have specified to a stranger, he should be able to walk into your classroom and decide if the objective is being reached. If the stranger's decision agrees with yours, then the objective has passed the stranger test.

For an objective to pass the *stranger test,* it must be specific. It must describe what the learner will be doing, his *behavior* when he meets the objective; it must describe the situation, the *setting* when the behavior is to occur; and finally, it must describe how well, or to what *criterion* the behavior is to be performed.

It is not enough to have your objectives "in mind." It is necessary to be more specific. -

Caution: Many people, when they first attempt to write teaching objectives, make the mistake of not clearly specifying a behavior. Instead, they attempt to use vague terms such as "the child will appreciate," "the child will like," "the child will understand," "the child will know," or "the child will develop a sense of." The problem, of course, is that these vague terms mean different things to different people. A vague term will not pass the *stranger test.* When you describe a behavior, it should be *observable, measurable,* and *clearly specified.*

Exercise

Place an X next to each of the following behaviors which are observable and measurable:
____ 1. the child will put away the blocks
____ 2. the child will enjoy
____ 3. the child will talk quietly
____ 4. the child will know
Place an X next to each of the following behaviors which are clearly specified:
____ 5. the child will comprehend
____ 6. the child will walk to the drinking fountain
____ 7. the child will hang up his coat
____ 8. the child will be nice

Answers: 1, 3, 6, 7.

Exercise

Below are several objectives. Read each objective and determine if:

1. It is complete, that is, the *setting*, *behavior*, and *criterion* are specified clearly and in detail.
2. The *setting* is not specified.
3. The *behavior* is vaguely stated.
4. The *criterion* is not specified.
5. More than one part is not specified or is vaguely stated.

Sample: When asked by the teacher to put away the toys he is playing with, the child will begin to put the toys away immediately and complete the task within five minutes.

SETTING:	When asked by the teacher to put away the toys he is playing with, the child will begin to
BEHAVIOR:	put the toys away
CRITERION:	immediately and complete the task within 5 minutes.

This objective is an example of No. __1__

A. During playtime the child will play.

SETTING:
BEHAVIOR:
CRITERION:

This objective is an example of No._____.

B. During story time the child will listen.

SETTING:
BEHAVIOR:
CRITERION:

This objective is an example of No._____.

C. When the child arrives at school in the morning, he will hang up his coat on the proper hook before he starts to play.

```
SETTING:
BEHAVIOR:
CRITERION:
```

This objective is an example of No._____.

D. The child will say "please" and "thank you" in a normal voice.

```
SETTING:
BEHAVIOR:
CRITERION:
```

This objective is an example of No._____.

E. During song time the child will learn to appreciate music.

```
SETTING:
BEHAVIOR:
CRITERION:
```

This objective is an example of No._____.

F. The child will look at a book for at least five minutes.

```
SETTING:
BEHAVIOR:
CRITERION:
```

This objective is an example of No._____.

Answers: A-4, B-4, C-1, D-2, E-5, F-2.

Exercise

Now write several of your own objectives for the children you are with. Include the *setting, behavior,* and *criterion.*

A._____

SETTING:
BEHAVIOR:
CRITERION:

B._____

SETTING:
BEHAVIOR:
CRITERION:

C._____

SETTING:
BEHAVIOR:
CRITERION:

D._____

SETTING:
BEHAVIOR:
CRITERION:

Try out your objectives by using the *stranger test.* If the objectives pass, you pass.

How To Evaluate Teaching
What To Look For

3

Observing Behavior
Landmarks

Earlier we stated that, "Teachers are people who change learners." This reflects a conviction that teaching has only taken place when learning has taken place. Occasionally, you will hear a parent or teacher say, "I've taught him to do this fifty times, but he still doesn't do it." What these "teachers" fail to recognize is that teaching is measured by the effect the teacher has on the learner. If a teacher attempts to teach a child to do something and after the attempt the child still cannot do it, the teacher has not taught it.

Teaching is the effect you have on the learner.

To improve your teaching, you must become aware of the effect you are having on the children you are attempting to teach. To see this effect, you must *evaluate* your teaching.

There are several ways to *evaluate* the effectiveness of your teaching.

● For some objectives, often all you will want to know is, "Does the child meet the objective?"

If you have specified your objective clearly and in detail, then *evaluation* becomes quite simple. Before you begin teaching, determine whether the child currently meets the objective you are interested in. To do this you must *observe* the child and see if the behavior called for in the objective occurs in the designated setting to the criterion specified. This is called a *pretest*. If the child is currently meeting the objective, then you do not need to teach it. If the child is not currently meeting the objective,

49

then you will need to teach it. To *evaluate* the effectiveness of your teaching, you continue to observe the child to see if he now meets the objective as a result of your teaching.

For example, Mary wants all of the children in her class to be able to tie their shoes. First, she specifies her objective:

SETTING:	Given a shoe with laces that are untied, the child will
BEHAVIOR:	tie the laces
CRITERION:	in a standard bowknot within 3 minutes without any help.

Next, Mary *pretests* all of the children to determine which children already meet this objective and which children she will need to teach. Mary then individually teaches those children who did not meet the objective. Mary continuously observes the children she is working with during the teaching process to determine their progress toward meeting the objective. When a child meets the objective, Mary knows that both the child and she have succeeded. Continuous observation during the teaching process provides much more information to the teacher than does a single observation after the teaching process. In fact, if we only observe once before and once after the teaching process, we may actually start going in the wrong direction during the teaching process and not realize it.

It is for this reason that Mary prefers to continuously evaluate the behavior of a child who she is teaching. Mary has found that this makes her a better teacher since at the same time she is teaching the child, the child is teaching her how to teach. The reason for this is that a change in a child's behavior toward meeting the objective she is teaching works as an accelerating consequence for Mary. By continuously evaluating she is immediately aware of the change in the child's behavior, and when it is in the direction of the objective she has specified, Mary's successful teaching behavior is speeded up.

If the child's behavior is not changing or is moving in the wrong direction, this acts as a decelerating consequence and slows down Mary's ineffective teaching behavior.

Teachers are also learners.

● For other objectives you will not only want to know if the child meets the objective, but also how often he meets the objective. When an objective specifies a behavior that is limited as to how often it can occur, such as "greeting in the morning," which can occur only once each day, or "answering questions," which can only occur if a question is asked, we *evaluate* by observing and counting the percent of time the child meets the objective when given the opportunity to meet the objective.

For example, Mary wants all of the children in her class to greet her in the morning. First, she specifies her objective:

SETTING:	When the child arrives at school, he will
BEHAVIOR:	say "good morning," "hello," or "hi"
CRITERION:	in a moderate voice when he first sees the teacher.

Mary selects George to work with. George knows how to and does occasionally greet Mary in the morning. What Mary must do is speed up his greeting her. Before she begins to speed up this behavior, she observes and counts it for a week. During this time George greets her one out of five mornings, or twenty percent of the time. Next, Mary begins to speed up his greeting behavior by praising him whenever he greets her in the morning. During the second week George greets her three out of five mornings, or sixty percent of the time, and by the third week George greets her five out of five mornings, or one hundred percent of the time.

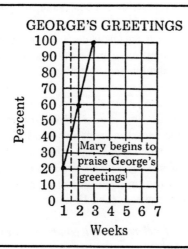

GEORGE'S GREETINGS

● For objectives which specify behaviors that are not limited as to how often they can occur, you will want to know the *rate* of the behavior.

When Mary is teaching a child, she is attempting to change his behavior to meet the objective she has specified. When the change in behavior requires either speeding up or slowing down a behavior that is not limited as to how often it can occur, Mary measures this change by determining the *rate* of the behavior before she starts teaching and the *rate* of the behavior during the time she is teaching. If the *rate* of the behavior is changing in the direction she has specified in her objective, she knows that she is being effective in her teaching.

Measuring Rate
Speedometer

To determine the *rate* of a behavior:

1. *Specify the behavior and the setting in which the behavior is to be observed.* Brady's hitting occurs at different rates in free play, song time, and juice and cookies. If you were trying to teach Brady not to hit and observed Brady's hitting in free play one day and during juice and cookies the next day, you might mistakenly assume that his hitting slowed down because of something you did when, in fact, his rate of hitting was always lower during juice and cookies than during free play. Therefore, always observe in a constant setting.

2. *Observe and count the behavior when it occurs.* You can do this by putting a mark on a piece of paper every time the behavior occurs, or by using a small counter such as golfers use to help keep track of their strokes.

3. *Measure the amount of time during which you observe and count the behavior.* All you need for this is a watch. Just record when you begin observing and when you stop. Then count the number of minutes you spent observing. You will find that this will work best if you decide on a specific time period and keep the amount of time you observe each day constant (i.e., 10 minutes, 20 minutes).

4. *Divide the number of behaviors that you counted by the number of minutes you spent observing.*

$$\frac{\text{Number of behaviors}}{\text{Number of minutes}} = \textit{Rate} \text{ per minute}$$

For example, Mary is interested in speeding up Randy's *rate* of putting blocks away during clean-up time. First, Mary clearly and in detail specifies the objective:

SETTING: During clean-up time, the child will

BEHAVIOR: put blocks away

CRITERION: in their appropriate place, at a RATE of 5 blocks per minute or greater, until all of the blocks are put away. This will be done quietly--either silently or talking in a moderate voice--walking, avoiding other children who might be in the way, hands and feet to himself.

Next, Mary observes Randy in a constant setting (block clean-up period), counts the number of blocks he puts away, and notes the amount of time spent in observation. Mary records this information on a Project Record Chart.

PROJECT RECORD CHART

CHILD'S NAME   *RANDY*   TEACHER'S NAME   *MARY*
SETTING   *During clean-up time, the child will*
BEHAVIOR   *put blocks away*
CRITERION   *in their appropriate place, at a RATE of 5 blocks per minute or greater, until all of the blocks are put away. This will be done quietly--either silently or talking in a moderate voice--walking, avoiding other children who might be in the way, hands and feet to himself.*

Date	Behav- iors	Start Time	Stop Time	Total Min.	Rate Per Min.	Comments
10/15	24	9:30	9:42	12	2.0	PRETEST

Since Randy put away twenty-four blocks in twelve minutes, Randy's *rate* of putting blocks away is:

$$\frac{24 \text{ blocks put away}}{12 \text{ minutes}} = \begin{array}{l} 2.0 \text{ blocks put away} \\ \text{per minute} \end{array}$$

Clearly Randy did not meet the objective Mary had established.

Determining Direction by Graphing Behavior
Compass

It is not enough to know the speed we are moving, that is, the *rate* of the behavior, we must also know the direction we are moving. Obviously, we need a compass.

To determine the direction in which a behavior is moving, we must observe more than once. Mary decided to observe and count Randy's behavior for three days *(pretest)* before she introduced a teaching program to speed up his behavior. Mary recorded this information on a Project Record Chart.

During this time his *rates* of putting blocks away were:

1st day	2.0 blocks put away per minute	
2nd day	3.1	"
3rd day	1.8	"

On the fourth day, Mary began her teaching program to speed up Randy's putting away blocks. Mary begins by praising Randy each time he puts a block away. Soon Mary only praises Randy following every other block he puts away, and later only after every fifth and then every tenth block he puts away. For the next seven school days Randy's *rates* of putting blocks away are:

4th day	2.2 blocks put away per minute	
5th day	3.8	"
6th day	4.9	"
7th day	3.7	"
8th day	5.6	"
9th day	8.0	"
10th day	7.4	"

PROJECT RECORD CHART

CHILD'S NAME *RANDY*   TEACHER'S NAME *MARY*
SETTING *During clean-up time, the child will*
BEHAVIOR *put blocks away*
CRITERION *in their appropriate place, at a RATE of 5 blocks per*
minute or greater, untill all of the blocks are put away.
This will be done quietly--either silently or talking in
a moderate voice--walking, avoiding other children who
might be in the way, hands and feet to himself.

Date	Behav-iors	Start Time	Stop Time	Total Min.	Rate Per Min.	Comments
10/15	24	9:30	9:42	12	2.0	⎫
10/16	31	9:25	9:35	10	3.1	⎬ Pretest
10/17	18	9:32	9:42	10	1.8	⎭
10/20	22	9:40	9:50	10	2.2	⎫
10/21	34	9:36	9:45	9	3.8	
10/22	59	9:28	9:40	12	4.9	Behavior
10/23	37	9:32	9:42	10	3.7	⎬ is
10/24	62	9:27	9:38	11	5.6	Praised
10/27	80	9:35	9:45	10	8.0	
10/28	81	9:29	9:40	11	7.4	⎭

In order to see how well she is teaching Randy to put away blocks, Mary *graphs* the *rate* of his block putting away behavior each day on a Project Behavior Graph. To do this, Mary puts a dot opposite the *rate* per minute of block putting away behavior that she observes each day, and then she connects the dots.

Here is what the graph looks like:

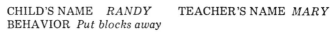

PROJECT BEHAVIOR GRAPH

CHILD'S NAME *RANDY*   TEACHER'S NAME *MARY*

BEHAVIOR *Put blocks away*

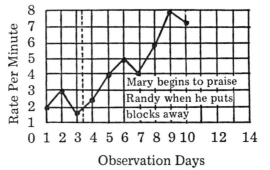

Observation Days

Even though Randy's block putting away behavior is not always greater each day than the day before, Mary can easily see with the aid of the graph that this behavior is moving in the right direction. The graph is Mary's compass; it tells her in which direction the behavior is moving.

Caution: A graph can only be as accurate as the *rate* information you collect each day. The less accurate the *rate* information, the more misleading your "compass" will be.

At the back of this book there are a number of blank Project Record Charts and Project Behavior Graphs for you to use. When carrying out a teaching program:

1. Fill out the Project Record Chart and Project Behavior Graph, including the child's name, teacher's name, *setting, behavior,* and *criterion.*

2. Each day record on the Project Record Chart, the date, behavior, starting time, stopping time, total minutes, and *rate* per minute.

3. Each day plot on the Project Behavior Graph the *rate* per minute of the behavior you are observing.

56

The vertical line on the left side of the Project Behavior Graphs provided at the back of the book is left blank. Each of the lines can stand for any number that best suits the *rate* of the behavior you are counting. For some of the behaviors you might count, the *rate* may be quite high, and the lines may be labeled 0, 10, 20, 30, 40, etc., whiie for others the *rate* of the behavior may be quite low, and the lines may be labeled 0, .1, .2, .3, .4, etc. Label the vertical lines so that you have room to plot all of the *rates* of the ′ behavior and so that you can readily see changes in the *rate*.

Exercise

Complete the Project Record Chart below by calculating the Total Minutes and Rate where they are missing.

PROJECT RECORD CHART

CHILD'S NAME *CAROL*   TEACHER'S NAME *MARY*
SETTING
BEHAVIOR
CRITERION

Date	Behav-iors	Start Time	Stop Time	Total Min.	Rate Per Min.	Comments
3/2	20	10:30	10:40	10	2.0	
3/3	20	10:35	10:45	10		Pretest
3/4	24	10:32	10:42			
3/5	18	10:30	10:39			
3/6	22	10:36	10:47			
3/9	26	10:31	10:39			
3/10	29	10:33	10:45			
3/11	34	10:38	10:50			Behavior
3/12	36	10:33	10:45			is
3/13	38	10:30	10:40			Praised
3/16	36	10:34	10:43			
3/17	41	10:31	10:42			
3/18	39	10:37	10:50			
3/19	40	10:34	10:44			

Teachers generally find it easier to start and stop at the same times each day and to observe for a constant period of time, for example, 10, 20, or 30 minutes.

You can graph the percent of time that a behavior occurs, just as you have graphed rate. See page 51 for an example.

Exercise

Complete the Project Behavior Graph below using the *rate* information from the Project Record Chart on the previous page.

PROJECT BEHAVIOR GRAPH

CHILD'S NAME   *CAROL*   TEACHER'S NAME   *MARY*
BEHAVIOR

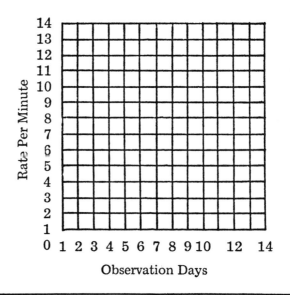

Common Pitfalls in Teaching
Why Some People Get Lost

Lack of Objectives
Some People Don't Know Where They Want to Go

Many teachers either don't know or they only have a vague idea of where they want to go. This is dangerous since you recall that:

> If you don't know where you want to go, you probably will not get to a place you would like to be.

When a teacher starts traveling without specifying a destination, it is easy for her to get lost.

A teacher can also get lost if she does not describe her objective clearly and in detail. If you start with a vague destination, you might reach that vicinity, but you probably will not get to exactly where you would like to be.

It is also ironic, but true, that if you do not know where you would like to go, you will never know if and when you've arrived.

Misuse of Consequences, Shaping, Cues, and Modeling
Some People Don't Know How to Travel

There are numerous mistakes you can make while traveling.

● Some teachers begin teaching without knowing how to speed up or slow down behaviors. How would you like to be in the driver's seat and not know the difference between the accelerator and the brake? Some teachers are in this position.

Example:
   Susan spends almost all of her time during preschool sitting by herself against a wall, watching the other children play. Several times each day Susan's teacher comes over to her and spends five to ten minutes talking to Susan in an effort to try to get her to join the other children in play activities. Susan continues to isolate herself each day.

SUSAN	
BEHAVIOR	
CONSEQUENCE	
EFFECT ON BEHAVIOR	

What behavior did Susan's teacher want to speed up? _____

What behavior was Susan's teacher actually maintaining? _____

● Some teachers don't provide accelerating consequences at all. These teachers go on the assumption that, "The child is supposed to be good," or "The child should learn for the sake of learning," or "That is what the child should be doing," without receiving any accelerating consequences for his behaviors. If you encounter a teacher who believes this (and there are some around), ask her how long she would continue to teach if she did not receive a paycheck or social approval for what she is doing.

   Remember—Things that are taken for granted often go away. If accelerating consequences are not provided, the behavior will slow down.

● Some teachers don't provide immediate consequences.

Example:
   Linda carefully puts away all of the toys she has been playing with and then starts running about. Linda's teacher wants to show that she is

60

pleased when Linda puts away the toys so she smiles and says, "Good, Linda," as Linda races by her. The next day Linda fails to put the blocks away after she plays with them; instead she starts running about.

LINDA	
BEHAVIOR	putting away toys
CONSEQUENCE	
EFFECT ON BEHAVIOR	

BEHAVIOR	running about
CONSEQUENCE	
EFFECT ON BEHAVIOR	

What behavior did Linda's teacher want to speed up? _____
_____

What behavior did Linda's teacher actually speed up? _____
_____

The mistake that Linda's teacher made was that the accelerating consequence did not _____
follow the behavior she wanted to speed up.

● Some teachers don't provide effective consequences.

Consequences may not be effective for several reasons:

Just because a consequence works as an accelerating consequence for one child does not necessarily mean that it will work as an accelerating consequence for another child.

A consequence may lose its effectiveness if it is overused. If a teacher frequently used the same accelerating consequence, such as, "Wow, that's great," it may become less and less effective.

A consequence may be too small. If a consequence is not large enough, it will not be effective. For some children a light touch will be effective as an accelerating consequence. For other children this consequence will be too small, and it will not be effective; however, for some of these children a hug will be effective as an accelerating consequence.

Remember—You must determine for each child what will work as an accelerating consequence.

A consequence may also be too large or too powerful. It is much more effective to present many small consequences to a child than a single large consequence. If large, powerful consequences are often presented, smaller, less powerful consequences will lose their effectiveness.

Remember—Don't use accelerating consequences that are more powerful than necessary to speed up the child's behavior. If praise works, don't use candy!

When praise is used as an accelerating consequence, it may not be effective unless it is directed at a specific behavior.

Remember—Always use descriptive praise, and praise the behavior, not the child.

● Some teachers don't consistently present an accelerating consequence immediately following the behavior every time the behavior occurs when they are trying to speed up a behavior that is just being learned.

Example:

Gretta's teacher decides that Gretta should learn to hang up her coat when she arrives at school in the morning. The next day the teacher shows Gretta how to hang up her coat. The following day when Gretta arrives at school, she hangs up her coat just as she was shown. The teacher sees Gretta and congratulates herself for having successfully taught Gretta this new behavior. Several days later the teacher sees Gretta dropping her coat on the floor rather than hanging it up. The teacher is puzzled because she recalls that she "successfully taught" Gretta to hang up her coat.

GRETTA	
BEHAVIOR	hanging up coat
CONSEQUENCE	
EFFECT ON BEHAVIOR	

What did the teacher do wrong? _____

_____

What should the teacher have done? _____

_____

● Some teachers present too many accelerating consequences when they are trying to maintain a behavior that is already learned.

Remember—Once a behavior is learned, it is more likely to be maintained if it is only occasionally followed by accelerating consequences.

● Some teachers accidentally speed up a behavior that they do not wish to speed up.

Example:
Jennifer "throws a tantrum" at school, and the teacher takes her aside and talks with her to find out what is bothering her. Jennifer's tantrums continue to occur.

JENNIFER	
BEHAVIOR	
CONSEQUENCE	
EFFECT ON BEHAVIOR	

What did the teacher do wrong? _____

_____

What should the teacher have done?_____

_____

Example:
Roberta often threatens to hit other children. Whenever this occurs, the teacher sets Roberta down to talk and "reasons" with her. Roberta's rate of threatening other children increases.

ROBERTA	
BEHAVIOR	
CONSEQUENCE	
EFFECT ON BEHAVIOR	

What did the teacher do wrong? _____

_____

What should the teacher have done? _____

_____

Exercise

See if you can catch yourself accidentally speeding up a behavior that you do not wish to speed up.

The behavior I was speeding up was: _____

_____

The accelerating consequence I was presenting was: _____

_____

● Some teachers accidentally slow down a behavior that they do not wish to slow down.

Example:

When Emily entered the preschool, she seemed to be a model child in the manner in which she shared and cooperated with the other children. During the first few weeks the teacher spent all of her time working with the children who seemed to be "problems" or seemed to have problems. After these first few weeks Emily no longer shared and cooperated with the other children. In fact, she started to display a number of problem behaviors. These problem behaviors continued to occur.

EMILY	
BEHAVIOR	sharing and cooperating
CONSEQUENCE	
EFFECT ON BEHAVIOR	

BEHAVIOR	problem behaviors
CONSEQUENCE	
EFFECT ON BEHAVIOR	

What did the teacher do wrong? _____

_____

What should the teacher have done? _____

_____

● Some teachers, when trying to slow down a behavior, eliminate the accelerating consequence that is maintaining the behavior, by ignoring the behavior when it occurs. However, they occasionally attend the child when the behavior occurs.

Example:
    Richard often whines over minor incidents like not being able to go first on the slide or dropping a toy. His teacher, who had been attending to him whenever he whined, decides to try to slow down Richard's whining by ignoring him whenever he whines. For the next several weeks the teacher ignores most of Richard's whining, although occasionally she goes over to him while he is whining to check if anything is really the matter. She reasons that as long as she ignores most of Richard's whining, it should go away. However, instead of slowing down, the rate of Richard's whining actually speeds up. The teacher decides that ignoring "doesn't work" and that she will have to start punishing Richard whenever he whines.

RICHARD	
BEHAVIOR	
CONSEQUENCE	
EFFECT ON BEHAVIOR	

What did the teacher do wrong? _____

_____

What should the teacher have done? _____

_____

> *Remember—If you do not consistently ignore an undesirable behavior, it will not slow down. By occasionally attending to the undesirable behavior, you may maintain it at a high rate.*

● Some teachers, when trying to quickly slow down a behavior, use social isolation as a means of eliminating all accelerating consequences. However, they sometimes do not really succeed in eliminating all accelerating consequences.

Example:
    Whenever Gregory hits another child, the teacher makes him go to the corner where the blocks are stacked and sit by himself. Gregory plays

65

with the blocks while he is in the corner. His rate of hitting other children actually increases.

GREGORY	
BEHAVIOR	
CONSEQUENCE	
EFFECT ON BEHAVIOR	

Remember—If all accelerating consequences are not eliminated, the behaviors will not slow down.

● Some teachers, when trying to quickly slow down a behavior, use social isolation as a means of eliminating all accelerating consequences. However, they use it too frequently.

Example:
Whenever Grant calls another child a name, the teacher makes Grant go sit by himself for several minutes. This happens an average of five to ten times a day. Initially, this procedure seemed to slow down the rate of Grant's name-calling. However, now it doesn't seem to have any effect at all. In fact, Grant's rate of name-calling increases.

GRANT	
BEHAVIOR	
CONSEQUENCE	
EFFECT ON BEHAVIOR	

What did the teacher do wrong? _____

What behavior is incompatible with name-calling? _____

What should the teacher have done? _____

Remember—The effectiveness of social isolation depends partly on its rarity. The less it is used, the more effective it will be.

● Some teachers, when trying to slow down a behavior, present a decelerating consequence without first trying other means of slowing down the behavior. These teachers often are not familiar with other means of slowing down a behavior and are not aware of the disadvantages of punishment.

● Some teachers, when trying to slow down a behavior, present what they think is a decelerating consequence but fail to observe its effect upon the behavior. This is particularly true of reprimands.

Remember—For some children reprimands not only don't slow down, but they actually speed up the rate of the behavior they immediately follow. The only way to know if a reprimand is a decelerating consequence for an individual child is to present the reprimand and observe whether the rate of the behavior that it immediately follows slows down, stays the same, or speeds up.

● Some teachers, when trying to slow down an undesirable behavior, fail to speed up desirable behaviors that are incompatible with the undesirable behavior.

Example:
Margaret gets her teacher's attention by asking questions in a very loud voice. The teacher decides to slow down this behavior by ignoring Margaret when she asks a question in a loud voice. However, the teacher also ignores Margaret when she asks a question in a moderate voice. Soon Margaret stops asking any questions at all.

MARGARET	
BEHAVIOR	asking questions in a loud voice
CONSEQUENCE	
EFFECT ON BEHAVIOR	
BEHAVIOR	asking questions in a moderate voice
CONSEQUENCE	
EFFECT ON BEHAVIOR	

What did the teacher do wrong? _____

What behavior is incompatible with asking questions in a loud voice?
_____

What should the teacher have done? _____

_____

● Some teachers, when trying to teach a new behavior, fail to break the learning down into small steps.

Example:

Edwin does not know how to print his name. The teacher decides that this is something that he should learn. She takes a sheet of paper, prints Edwin's name at the top, gives him a pencil and the sheet of paper, and tells him to practice copying his name. After several minutes the teacher returns and notices that Edwin has not been successful in copying his name. She concludes that Edwin is not yet "ready" to learn this behavior and that she will just wait until he "matures" before she will try to "teach" him to print his name.

EDWIN	
BEHAVIOR	
CONSEQUENCE	
EFFECT ON BEHAVIOR	

What did the teacher do wrong? _____

What should the teacher have done? _____

_____

Remember—Break learning down into small steps that start where the child's behavior currently is and move toward where you want the child's behavior to go (destination).

● Some teachers, when trying to teach a new behavior, fail to present accelerating consequences immediately following each behavior that is a step closer to the destination.

Example:
James asks his teacher to show him how to tie his shoelaces. James' teacher knows that there are several steps involved in learning to tie shoelaces. She starts by demonstrating the first step for him and then leaves to let him practice. After he has practiced for a while, she returns and demonstrates the second step for him and then leaves again to let him practice some more. When she returns to show him the third step, James is no longer practicing, and when she tries to show him the third step, he says that he doesn't want to learn to tie his shoes.

JAMES	
BEHAVIOR	
CONSEQUENCE	
EFFECT ON BEHAVIOR	

What did the teacher do wrong? _____
_____
What should the teacher have done? _____
_____

● Some teachers, when trying to teach a new behavior, fail to present accelerating consequences only for those behaviors that are closer and closer to the destination.

Example:
Bobby is learning how to catch a ball. Whenever his teacher throws him the ball, the teacher praises Bobby whether he catches the ball or not. Bobby just doesn't seem to make much progress in learning to catch a ball well.

BOBBY	
BEHAVIOR	catching ball
CONSEQUENCE	
EFFECT ON BEHAVIOR	

BEHAVIOR	dropping ball
CONSEQUENCE	
EFFECT ON BEHAVIOR	

What did the teacher do wrong? _____

What should the teacher have done? _____

● Some teachers, when trying to teach a new behavior, fail to continue to raise the criterion for the presentation of accelerating consequences until they reach the destination.

Example:
Cindy has learned how to play "Mary Had a Little Lamb" on the piano. Cindy's teacher and her parents are so impressed that they strongly praise Cindy every time she plays this tune. At the end of the year Cindy still only knows how to play one tune, "Mary Had a Little Lamb," on the piano.

CINDY	
BEHAVIOR	
CONSEQUENCE	
EFFECT ON BEHAVIOR	

70

What did Cindy's teacher and parents do wrong? _____

What should they have done? _____

● Some teachers serve as models for undesirable behaviors.

Example:
    Jeff's teacher always shouts, "Everyone listen," when she wants to get the children's attention. Jeff and the other children in the class no longer talk in a moderate voice while playing as they did when they first entered school. Now they frequently shout to and at each other during playtime. Jeff's teacher also shouts more now, because the classroom is so noisy that it is difficult to get the children's attention.

JEFF	
CUE	
BEHAVIOR	
CONSEQUENCE	
EFFECT ON BEHAVIOR	

What did the teacher do wrong? _____

What should the teacher have done? _____

Remember—People often behave like other people they see.

● Some teachers present cues that start undesirable behaviors.

Example:
    Janet's teacher notices a few children acting restless during rest period and announces, "You can move around and talk during rest period

as long as you do it quietly." Soon all of the children in the room are moving about and talking, and no one is resting any longer. The activity and noise continue to increase to the point where the teacher announces, "You children did not listen to what I said. Now you will have to lie down and be quiet."

JANET	
CUE	"You can move around and talk during rest period."
BEHAVIOR	
CONSEQUENCE	
EFFECT ON BEHAVIOR	

What did the teacher do wrong? _____

_____

What should the teacher have done? _____

_____

● Some teachers present cues that are inconsistent, ambiguous, or vague.

Examples:

(Inconsistent) On the first day of school Laurie's teacher tells all of the children, "We always put away all of our toys during clean-up time before we go home." The next day the teacher announces, "It's clean-up time, but you can keep playing since you are playing so well."

(Ambiguous) Darla's teacher sees her take a truck that Jimmy is playing with when he was not looking. The teacher is quite amused since it is usually Jimmy that takes Darla's toys; however, she goes over to Darla and says with a big smile, "You shouldn't take the truck Jimmy is playing with."

(Vague) Robbie's teacher says, "I want you to be nice to each other."

72

Lack of Evaluation
Some People Don't Look Where They Are Going

Teachers often get lost because they don't look where they are going. Good teachers evaluate before, during, and after teaching, that is to say, they evaluate continuously. This may consist of:

● Simply determining if the child meets the objective. We do this by specifying the objective and then observing the child to see if the behavior called for in the objective occurs in the designated setting to the criterion specified. This *pretest* will show whether the child is currently meeting the objective or not. If the child is not currently meeting the objective, you begin teaching and continue to observe the child to see if he now meets the objective as a result of your teaching.

● Determining, for an objective that specifies a behavior that is limited as to how often it can occur, the percent of time the child meets the objective when given the opportunity to meet the objective before, during, and after the teaching process.

● Determining, for an objective that specifies a behavior that is not limited as to how often it can occur, the *rate* of the behavior before, during, and after the teaching process. This consists of:

1. Specifying the behavior that is observable and measurable, and the setting in which it is to occur.

2. Observing and counting the behavior when it occurs.

3. Measuring the amount of time spent observing and counting the behavior.

4. Finding the *rate* of the behavior by dividing the number of behaviors counted by the number of minutes spent observing.

5. Graphing the *rate.*

Being A Good Teacher
How To Travel Without Getting Lost

5

Principle One: Pretest
Find Out Where You Are

Following a terrible storm, the captain of a luxury liner bound for Liverpool from New York called his passengers up on deck and announced, "I've got some bad news and some good news to tell you. The bad news is that we're absolutely lost. We haven't any idea where we are. Our electronic compass has gone on the blink. We've lost all radio contact with the mainland. Because of the overcast conditions, we aren't able to use celestial navigation. We are hopelessly lost. Now for the good news. We are two hours ahead of schedule." At that moment the ship struck land at the tip of Greenland and ran ashore.

What mistake did the captain make? The captain's objectives were quite clear; he knew exactly where he wanted to go. He also was very familiar with his ship and knew how to travel. Obviously, his mistake was that he was traveling without knowing where he was. Knowing precisely where you are before you start to travel has long been recognized as important to navigation. Unfortunately, its importance often goes unrecognized in education. For many years educators have been trying to move students from point A to point B without ever determining precisely where point A is.

Find out where you are before you start to travel. You may already be where you want to be.

In order to know what to start teaching a child, you must first determine what the child is currently able to do. You do this by a *pretest*.

Principle Two: Define Objectives
Specify Where You Want to Go

To avoid getting lost, you must always specify your objectives clearly and in detail.

Do this by asking yourself:
What behavior do I want the learner to perform?
In what *setting* do I want the behavior to occur?
How well, or to what *criterion*, do I want the behavior to be performed?

Then see if your objective passes the *stranger test.*

Principle Three: Design and Carry Out A Teaching Program
Plan A Trip and Start Traveling

By now you already know all you need to know to design and carry out a teaching program. Below is a sample teaching program presented in a convenient form that you can use to help organize your teaching programs.

First, write a description of what you would like to teach.

Task Description:
When a child asks for something that he would like, he will say "please," and when a child receives something that he likes, whether he asks for it or not, he will say "thank you."

Second, write specific objectives based upon the task description.

Specific Objectives:

SETTING:	When a child asks for something that he would like, he will
BEHAVIOR:	say "please"
CRITERION:	in the sentence or immediately following the sentence carrying the request, in a moderate voice, without the teacher providing cues such as "remember to say 'please.'"
SETTING:	When a child receives something that he likes, he will
BEHAVIOR:	say "thank you"
CRITERION:	within 30 seconds of receiving whatever it was that he was given, in a moderate voice, without the teacher providing cues such as "remember to say 'thank you.'"

Third, list the behaviors you wish to accelerate and those you wish to decelerate.

Accelerate

Saying "please" and "thank you" at appropriate times.

Saying "please" and "thank you" in a moderate voice.

Saying "please" and "thank you" without the teacher providing cues.

Asking for something that he would like.

Decelerate

Saying "please" and "thank you" at inappropriate times.

Saying "please" and "thank you" too softly or too loudly.

Saying "please" and "thank you" when given a cue by the teacher.

Grabbing, taking by force, demanding, threatening, whining.

Fourth, *pretest* the child to determine if and how often he meets the objectives.

Fifth, develop a *Teaching Unit* by listing the *behaviors* you wish to start, speed up, or slow down; the *cues* you will provide; and the *consequences* you will present.

As you carry out a teaching program, you will want to gradually stop providing cues and to maintain the behavior by presenting accelerating consequences when the behavior occurs.

Exercise

Design a teaching program. List the task description, specify the objectives, and list the behaviors to accelerate and decelerate. Pretest the children and then write a Teaching Unit.

Carry out the training program and evaluate it by determining the child's progress in meeting the objective(s).

Principle Four: Evaluate Continuously
Look Where You Are Going

In order to travel anywhere, you must look where you are going. To do this, you need to observe your progress each day. This may consist of:

1. Simply noting if the child now meets the objectives you have specified;
2. Determining what percent of the time the child meets the objective when given the opportunity to meet the objective; or
3. Measuring the *rate* of the behavior and recording and graphing this information on Project Record Charts and Project Behavior Graphs.

Principle Five: Modify Teaching Programs
Adjust Your Travel Plans if Necessary

Occasionally, when you're traveling, you will find that you are not making any progress, or that you are progressing too slowly. Since you are

TEACHING UNIT

MARK	
CUE	"WHEN YOU WANT SOMETHING, ask for it and say 'please.' I'll show you. Mark *please* hand me the puzzle."
BEHAVIOR	Mark hands puzzle to teacher.
CONSEQUENCE	"Thank you."
CUE	"Let's practice. Ask me for the puzzle."
BEHAVIOR	"Will you please hand me the puzzle?"
CONSEQUENCE	Hand puzzle to Mark and say, "You remembered to say please."
CUE	"Mark, please hand me the puzzle."
BEHAVIOR	Mark hands puzzle to teacher.
CONSEQUENCE	"Thank you."
CUE	"Did you hear me say 'thank you' when you gave me the puzzle?"
BEHAVIOR	"Yes."
CONSEQUENCE	"Good listening."
CUE	"WHEN SOMEONE GIVES YOU SOMETHING, what do you say?"
BEHAVIOR	"Thank you."
CONSEQUENCE	"That's right."
CUE	"Let's practice. Ask me for the puzzle."
BEHAVIOR	"Will you please hand me the puzzle?"
CONSEQUENCE	Hand puzzle to Mark.
CUE	Mark receives puzzle.
BEHAVIOR	"Thank you."
CONSEQUENCE	"Great, you remembered to say 'thank you.'"

continuously evaluating you will know this immediately. When this happens you should check to see if you are making any of the mistakes we discussed in the last chapter that cause teachers to get lost. If you find a mistake, correct it; if you cannot find a mistake, you will have to adjust your travel plans by either changing the *cues* provided, the *behaviors* required, or the *consequences* presented. Since you are continuously evaluating your progress, you will be able to observe the effects of any adjustments you may make. Keep adjusting until you are able to make progress.

If the child's behavior is not changing in the direction you would like, it is not the fault of the child. It is the fault of the teaching program. Change the teaching program until it works.

How To be a Good Teacher on Five Principles Every Day

1. *Find out where you are*
   Pretest

2. *Specify where you want to go*
   Define objectives

3. *Plan a trip and start traveling*
   Design and carry out a teaching program

4. *Look where you are going*
   Evaluate continuously

5. *Adjust your travel plans if necessary*
   Modify teaching programs

PROJECT RECORD CHART

CHILD'S NAME _____TEACHER'S NAME _____

SETTING _____

BEHAVIOR _____

CRITERION _____

Date	Behaviors	Start Time	Stop Time	Total Min.	Rate Per Min.	Comments

PROJECT BEHAVIOR GRAPH

CHILD'S NAME _____ TEACHER'S NAME _____

BEHAVIOR _____

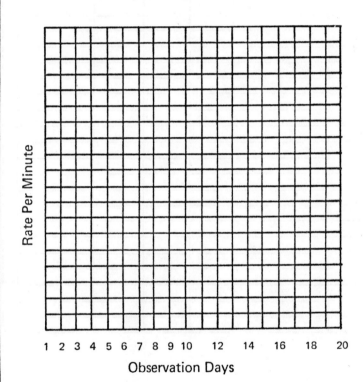

Rate Per Minute

1 2 3 4 5 6 7 8 9 10   12   14   16   18   20

Observation Days

PROJECT RECORD CHART

CHILD'S NAME _____ TEACHER'S NAME _____

SETTING _____

BEHAVIOR _____

CRITERION _____

Date	Behaviors	Start Time	Stop Time	Total Min.	Rate Per Min.	Comments

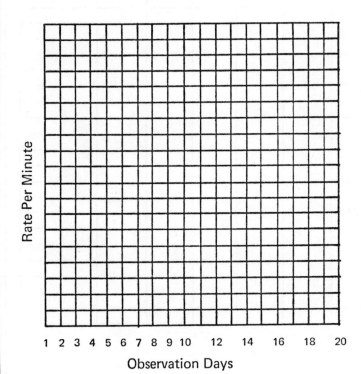

PROJECT BEHAVIOR GRAPH

CHILD'S NAME _____ TEACHER'S NAME _____

BEHAVIOR _____

Rate Per Minute

1 2 3 4 5 6 7 8 9 10 12 14 16 18 20

Observation Days

PROJECT RECORD CHART

CHILD'S NAME _____ TEACHER'S NAME _____

SETTING _____

BEHAVIOR _____

CRITERION _____

Date	Behaviors	Start Time	Stop Time	Total Min.	Rate Per Min.	Comments

PROJECT BEHAVIOR GRAPH

CHILD'S NAME _____ TEACHER'S NAME _____

BEHAVIOR _____

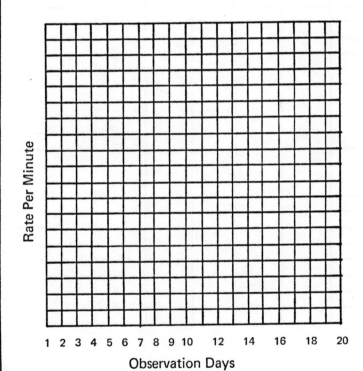

Rate Per Minute

1 2 3 4 5 6 7 8 9 10   12   14   16   18   20

Observation Days

PROJECT RECORD CHART

CHILD'S NAME _____TEACHER'S NAME _____
SETTING _____
BEHAVIOR _____
CRITERION _____

Date	Behaviors	Start Time	Stop Time	Total Min.	Rate Per Min.	Comments

PROJECT BEHAVIOR GRAPH

CHILD'S NAME _____ TEACHER'S NAME _____

BEHAVIOR _____

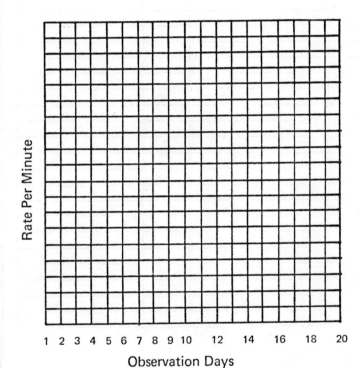

Rate Per Minute

1 2 3 4 5 6 7 8 9 10   12   14   16   18   20

Observation Days

PROJECT RECORD CHART

CHILD'S NAME _____ TEACHER'S NAME _____

SETTING _____

BEHAVIOR _____

CRITERION _____

Date	Behav-iors	Start Time	Stop Time	Total Min.	Rate Per Min.	Comments

PROJECT BEHAVIOR GRAPH

CHILD'S NAME _____ TEACHER'S NAME _____

BEHAVIOR _____

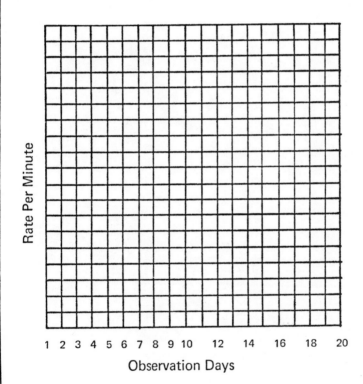

Rate Per Minute

1 2 3 4 5 6 7 8 9 10   12   14   16   18   20

Observation Days